THIS BOOK BELONGS TO:

NAME: ....

PHONE: ....

IF FOUND PLEASE:

☐ Return   ☐ Read   ☐ Burn   ☐ Use

DRAW YOUR SELF-PORTRAIT WITH EYES CLOSED

IT IS WHAT IT IS

Love conquers all

Feel the fear and do it anyway

When nothing goes right, go left.

Impossible is for the unwilling.

A day without sunshine is like, you know, night ^^

I would rather die on my feet than live on my knees

It's okay to not be okay as long as you are not giving up

Try Again. Fail again. Fail better

I bet giraffes don't even know what farts smell like

Every moment matters

When it rains look for rainbows

My life is my argument

Follow your heart

Nothing is worth more than this day

Keep it cool

Prove them wrong

Never stop dreaming

Love more. Worry less

Enjoy today

You are stronger than you think you are

You are somebody's reason to smile

Keep going. Be all in

Every noble work is at first impossible

Don't dream your life, live your dream

Do it with passion or not at all

The best is yet to come

If you're going through hell, keep going

Dream big. Pray bigger

If you want it, work for it

Good things happen to those who hustle

Begin now!

Choose to shine.

The past does not equal the future

We were born to be real, not to be perfect

Each day provides its own gifts

The two most important days in your life are the day you are born and they day you find out why

To the world you may be one person, but to one person you are the world

Actually, you can

I've got to keep breathing. It'll be my worst business mistake if I don't

I drive way too fast to worry about cholesterol

Slow down

Live the moment

Yes! Yes! You can do it!

Go forth on your path, as it exists only through your walking

Be who you needed when you were young

Take the risk or lose the chance

Be happy. Be bright. Be you

Darling, you are a work of art

I never feel more alone than when I'm trying to put sunscreen on my back

Stay foolish to stay sane

Time is the soul of this world

Now, is all you have

It is what it is

Don't let yesterday take up too much of today

Collect moments not things

You smile, I smile. That's how it works

It takes a long time to become young

Grow through what you go through

By the way, I'm wearing the smile you gave me

The eyes are useless when the mind is blind

Work hard. Stay humble

Do it.With love

No pressure, no diamonds

No rain. No flowers

Keep going

It does not matter how slowly you go
as long as you do not stop

You make mistakes. Mistakes don't make you

Leave no stone unturned

Believe you can and you're halfway there

Everything is going to be okay in the end. If it's
not the okay, it's not the end

Every day is a second chance

Don't rush things

The last woman I was in was the Statue of Liberty ^^

The wisest mind has something yet to learn

You are doing great

You can do anything you set your mind to

You are amazing. As you are. Stronger than you know. More beautiful than you think

Stars can't shine without darkness

Persistence guarantees that results are inevitable

Breathe

Sadness flies away on the wings of time

Forgiveness is giving up hope for a better past

You are amazing. Remember that

Every novel is a mystery novel if you never finish it

Whatever you do, do with all your might

You are capable of amazing things

The key to eating healthy is not eating any food that has a TV commercial

Every day may not be good but there is something good in every day

Just when I discovered the meaning of life, they changed it

You can if you think you can

Don't go through life, grow through life

We can do anything we want to if we stick to it long enough

At the end of hardship comes happiness

Breathe. It's just a bad day, not a bad life

Keep moving forward

Focus on the good

Choose happy

Made in the USA
Monee, IL
27 February 2022

91983522R00057